TREASURE TREATS
Leader Manual

Bible Adventure

Loveland, Colorado

Treasure Treats Leader Manual
Copyright © 1999 Group Publishing, Inc.

All rights reserved. No part of this book may be reproduced in any manner whatsoever without prior written permission from the publisher, except where noted on handouts and in the case of brief quotations embodied in critical articles and reviews. For information, write Permissions, Group Publishing, Inc., Dept. PD, P.O. Box 481, Loveland, CO 80539.

Credits
Treasure Hunt Bible Adventure Coordinator: Jody Brolsma
Author: Beth Rowland
Chief Creative Officer: Joani Schultz
Copy Editor: Pamela Shoup
Art Director: Kari K. Monson
Computer Graphic Artist: Randy Kady
Cover Art Director: Lisa Chandler
Cover Designers: Becky Hawley and Jerry Krutar
Cover Photographer: Craig DeMartino
Illustrator: Amy Bryant
Rain Forest Art: Pat Allen
Rain Forest Art Photographer: Linda Bohm
Production Manager: Peggy Naylor

Unless otherwise noted, Scripture taken from the HOLY BIBLE, NEW INTERNATIONAL VERSION®. Copyright © 1973, 1978, 1984 by International Bible Society. Used by permission of Zondervan Publishing House. All rights reserved.

ISBN 0-7644-9910-6
Printed in the United States of America.
10 9 8 7 6 5 4 3 2 1   00 99

CONTENTS

Welcome to Treasure Hunt Bible Adventure! 5

Your Contribution to
   Treasure Hunt Bible Adventure 6

The Overview 10

Gearing Up for the Adventure! 12

DAY 1 (The Bible shows us the way to trust.) 16

DAY 2 (The Bible shows us the way to love.) 21

DAY 3 (The Bible shows us the way to pray.) 25

DAY 4 (The Bible shows us the way to Jesus.) 31

DAY 5 (The Bible shows us the way to live.) 35

Welcome to TREASURE HUNT BIBLE ADVENTURE!

X marks the spot...for VBS excitement! Grab your compass, dust off your binoculars, and be sure your flashlight has batteries. You're hot on the trail to Treasure Hunt Bible Adventure, where kids discover Jesus—the greatest treasure of all! Your young adventurers will explore how the Bible maps the way to amazing riches, showing us the way to trust, love, pray, and live.

Kids will swing to captivating Bible songs during Treasure Hunt Sing & Play, join with their Clue Crews to monkey around at Jungle Gym Games, view *Chadder's Treasure Hunt Adventure* video, dig into Bible Exploration, create cool treasures at Craft Cave, and, of course, experience "vine" dining at Treasure Treats!

Treasure Treats is just one of seven Discovery Sites kids will visit each day at Treasure Hunt Bible Adventure. At each Discovery Site, kids will experience the daily Bible Point in a new way. During Treasure Treats, a select group of kids will serve the rest of their Clue Crew friends by making fun treats that tie in to each day's Bible Point.

Leading Treasure Treats is easy and fun!

You'll enjoy your role and be most successful as Treasure Treats Leader if you
- enjoy cooking and food preparation,
- have the ability to give clear directions to children,
- believe children can accomplish big things through help and cooperation,
- are accepting and supportive of children's abilities, and
- model God's love in everything you say and do.

Your Contribution

A CLUE FOR YOU!

It may be helpful to meet with the Treasure Hunt Director and go over the supply list. Let the director know what supplies you have or can collect on your own and what supplies you'll need to purchase or collect from church members. Open communication makes your job even easier!

Your Contribution to TREASURE HUNT BIBLE ADVENTURE

Here's what's expected of you before, during, and after Group's Treasure Hunt Bible Adventure:

Before TREASURE HUNT BIBLE ADVENTURE

♣ Attend scheduled Discovery Site Leader training.

♣ Pray for the kids who will attend your church's Treasure Hunt Bible Adventure.

♣ Ask your Treasure Hunt Director (otherwise known as your VBS Coordinator) what you should wear each day. Discovery Site Leader T-shirts (available from Group Publishing and your local Christian bookstore) help kids identify you—and help you identify other Discovery Site Leaders. If your Treasure Hunt Director doesn't order T-shirts, you may want to agree on another easily recognizable uniform, such as khaki shorts, a tan "explorers" vest, and hiking boots. For an added "culinary" effect, paper chefs hats are also available from Group Publishing and your local Christian bookstore.

♣ Read this Treasure Treats Leader Manual.

♣ Work with the Treasure Hunt Director to purchase or collect food and paper supplies. The Treasure Hunt Director Manual includes a photocopiable supply list you can put in your church bulletin to encourage church members to donate supplies.

♣ Meet with the Treasure Time Finale Leader. Each day's Treasure Time Finale will be a fun, involving review of the day's Bible story. The Finale Leader will need all Discovery Site Leaders on hand to make things go smoothly. Be prepared to assist with distributing, displaying, or collecting props as needed.

♣ Meet with the Jungle Gym Games Leader to go over your daily routine. Except for Day 1, the Games Leader will greet the kids on your Treasure Treats Service Crew, stay with the kids, and serve as your helper during Treasure Treats service. On Day 1 the preschoolers will be making the treats, so the Preschool Bible Treasure Land Leader will be your helper.

♣ Depending on how many kids you're expecting, you may want to recruit an assistant chef (in addition to the Games Leader). This person could be a

Field Test Findings

At our pilot program, the Treasure Treats Leader ended up with lots of helpers. Everyone from the church kitchen coordinator to the teenage sound technicians wanted to lend a hand. Consider recruiting the Treasure Hunt Sing & Play Leader or the Treasure Time Finale Leader to help out. They'll have a blast!

teenager, senior citizen, or VBS parent. No preparation is necessary—you can even invite a different helper each day!

♣ Prepare a snack setup site for each Clue Crew working in Treasure Treats. You can expect one-fourth of your church's total number of Clue Crews to report for Treasure Treats service each day (except for Day 1). A snack setup site consists of a round or rectangular table, necessary supplies for the day, a trash bag or trash can, plastic gloves, and stacks of dry and damp paper towels. Crews will work at their sites to prepare treats for everyone. Be sure to have lots of room between setup sites so kids can move around freely.

♣ Set up the dining area for other Clue Crews. If you're using long, rectangular tables, set up one table for every two crews (six people each). If you're using round tables, each crew may need its own table. If possible, set up the tables along the walls, as shown below. Post crew numbers on the tables or on nearby walls. Be sure to place *several* large trash cans where kids can easily deposit their trash!

When kids arrive, have them sit with their crews on the floor in the center of the room. After you introduce the Treasure Treats Service Crews, have kids thank and applaud them. Invite one of the children who prepared treats to explain the snack and how it teaches the Bible Point. Have a Prayer Person lead a prayer for the entire Treasure Hunt Bible Adventure. Then invite Clue Crews to go to their tables and enjoy!

A Clue for You!

If you don't have enough tables to accommodate all your Clue Crews, set up several serving tables, then post numbers on the walls around your room. Kids can pick up their treats from the serving tables, then sit on the floor near their crew numbers as they eat.

Field Test Findings

We didn't want kids to eat on the church's carpeted gymnasium floor (the colored whipped topping, strawberry cream cheese, and frosting were just a few red flags!). So we set the treats on two tables at the tiled entryway. Kids filed through, picked up their treats, and ate outside. The birds enjoyed the leftover crumbs, and the leaders enjoyed the minimal cleanup!

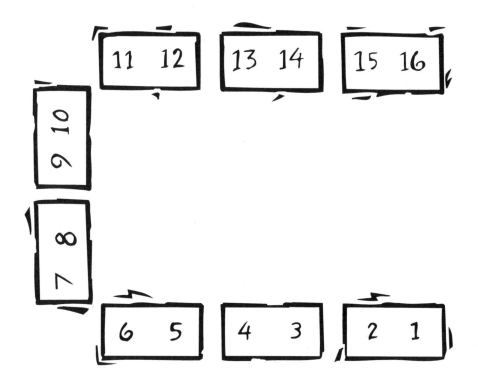

Your Contribution

Kids and Clue Crew Leaders aren't the only ones who get hungry! You may want to provide coffee, muffins, fruit, juice, or cinnamon rolls for Discovery Site Leaders to enjoy. They'll appreciate the time for rest and refreshment during a busy, active day.

STOP! READ ME FIRST!

You may be skeptical about kids making treats for the entire VBS. Believe it or not, they can do it! In Treasure Hunt Bible Adventure pilot programs, even preschoolers were able to make treats in the allotted time.

Before you decide to make alternative snack arrangements, consider the following reminders:

● Pray before each VBS day that snack preparation will go smoothly.

● Follow the setup and preparation instructions in this leader guide. Remember—they've been field-tested and revised for quick and easy snack-making.

● It's OK if kids' treats don't look perfect. The hungry kids who visit Treasure Treats each day won't even notice!

THEY CAN DO IT! Don't rob kids of the joy of serving others by doing their work ahead of time. We've heard from numerous VBS leaders who were reluctant to carry out this service idea. But when the week was over, they discovered that making treats for everyone became a great way to show love that kids viewed as a highlight of the week. And remember that if kids don't finish preparing the treats in the allotted time, you still have twenty-five minutes to finish up before kids arrive to eat.

During TREASURE HUNT BIBLE ADVENTURE

Treasure Treats Service

♣ Welcome each Clue Crew to Treasure Treats. Refer to Clue Crews as the Treasure Treats Service Crew, and tell them they're doing Treasure Treats service. Explain that by serving others, we can help them see the treasure of God's love. You'll have a new Treasure Treats Service Crew each day. The Jungle Gym Games Leader will also assist during Treasure Treats service (except for the first day when the Preschool Bible Treasure Land Leader will be your helper).

♣ Follow the snack preparation steps outlined in this leader manual. These procedures have been tested and retested to ensure a speedy, successful Treasure Treats service each day.

♣ Explain the snack preparation steps *before* kids meet at their snack setup sites so they won't be distracted by the food and preparation items. Tie the snack to the day's Point or Bible story.

♣ Have the games leader prepare drinks as you're explaining the snack preparation.

♣ To help create a fun atmosphere and reinforce Bible learning, play the *Treasure Hunt Sing & Play* audiocassette as the Treasure Treats crew prepares the snack.

♣ Help kids find jobs they can do well. If a child is having trouble with a task, suggest that he or she try a different one.

♣ Encourage kids' efforts and let them know the importance of their work—they're feeding the *entire* Treasure Hunt Bible Adventure! That's a lot of hungry explorers!

♣ Repeat the daily Bible Point often. It's important to say the Bible Point just as it's written. Repeating the Bible Point over and over will help children remember it and apply it to their lives. Kids will be listening for the Point each day so they can shout "Eureka!" Each day's Treasure Treats session suggests ways to include the Bible Point.

♣ When kids finish, have them deliver snack trays to the Preschool Bible Treasure Land. Choose a volunteer to explain to the younger children how the snack ties into the story or Bible Point.

♣ The Treasure Time Finale Leader may ask you to distribute Treasure Chest Quest Clues to your Treasure Treats Service Crew. If so, you'll receive an envelope of clues to distribute to the Clue Keeper in each Clue Crew. When your Treasure Treats Service Crew leaves, give the remaining clues to the Jungle Gym Games Leader. He or she will need to distribute them as other Clue Crews rotate through.

Treasure Treats

♣ Introduce the Treasure Treats Service Crew to the entire VBS. Have all the Cheerleaders lead everyone in cheering for the Treasure Treats crew.

♣ Have a Treasure Treats crew member explain how the snack ties into the story or the Bible Point.

♣ Have a Treasure Treats crew member lead everyone in a prayer of thanks for the food.

♣ Invite kids to pick up and enjoy their treats.

♣ After Treasure Treats, clean up the Treasure Treats area and set up as much as possible for the next day.

♣ Attend and participate in each day's Treasure Time Finale.

After TREASURE HUNT BIBLE ADVENTURE

♣ Thoroughly clean the Treasure Treats area—sweep and mop floors, wipe counter tops, and put tables away. Arrange for leftover food to be taken to a food bank or homeless shelter.

♣ Keep kids excited about their "treasure hunt" all year by
- phoning neighborhood kids who participated in your Treasure Hunt Bible Adventure program,
- sending Treasure Hunt Bible Adventure follow-up postcards, and
- having kids fix a Treasure Treats snack for the entire congregation.

A Clue For You!

The kids who do Treasure Treats Service would normally do Jungle Gym Games. That's why it's important that you give remaining Treasure Chest Quest Clues to the Jungle Gym Games Leader. If you keep the Clues, the rest of the kids who come to Jungle Gym Games won't receive one. Get it?

A Clue For You!

In a crowded room full of hungry kids, it can be hard to hear the person praying. Consider setting up a sound system in your snack area so everyone can hear the prayer and snack explanation.

▼▼ TREASURE HUNT BIBLE ADVENTURE OVERVIEW ▼▼

This is what everyone else is doing! At the Treasure Hunt Bible Adventure, the daily Bible Point is carefully integrated into each Discovery Site activity to reinforce Bible learning. Treasure Treats activities are an important part of kids' overall learning experience.

	BIBLE POINT	BIBLE STORY	BIBLE VERSE	TREASURE HUNT SING & PLAY	CRAFT CAVE	JUNGLE GYM GAMES
DAY 1	The Bible shows us the way to trust.	Peter walks to Jesus on the Sea of Galilee (Matthew 14:22-33).	"Do not let your hearts be troubled. Trust in God" (John 14:1a).	● He's Got the Whole World in His Hands ● The B-I-B-L-E ● Where Do I Go? ● I've Found Me a Treasure (chorus and verse 1)	**Craft** Jungle Gel **Application** Kids need to trust the Craft Cave Leader that Jungle Gel really works. In the same way, we need to trust God when things in life seem impossible.	**Games** ● Swamp Squish ● Peter's Windy Walk ● The River Bend ● Treasure Tag ● Pass-Along Peter **Application** The Bible teaches us that God is powerful and that we can trust him.
DAY 2	The Bible shows us the way to love.	Jesus washes the disciples' feet (John 13:1-17).	"A new command I give you: Love one another" (John 13:34a).	● Put a Little Love in Your Heart ● I've Found Me a Treasure (add verse 2) ● Jesus Loves Me	**Craft** Operation Kid-to-Kid Magnetic Bible Bookmarks **Application** Just as the magnet links the two children on the bookmark together, the Bible connects us with others around the world.	**Games** ● Monkeys Love Bananas ● Footrace ● Gold Coin Keep-Away ● Firefly Fling ● Mosquito Net **Application** As the Bible shows us how to love, we can love others.
DAY 3	The Bible shows us the way to pray.	Jesus prays for his disciples and all believers, and then he is arrested (John 17:1–18:11).	"I pray also for those who will believe in me through their message, that all of them may be one" (John 17:20a-21b).	● Let Us Pray ● Hey Now ● I've Found Me a Treasure (add verse 3)	**Craft** Surprise Treasure Chests **Application** When kids open the treasure chest, they'll be surprised at the "riches" inside. When we open our hearts to God in prayer, we'll be surprised by his loving response.	**Games** ● Savor the Flavor ● Centipede Scurry ● Message Mime ● It's a Jungle! ● Flowers of Blessing **Application** It's easy to talk to God.
DAY 4	The Bible shows us the way to Jesus.	Jesus is crucified, rises again, and appears to Mary Magdalene (John 19:1–20:18).	"For God so loved the world that he gave his one and only Son, that whoever believes in him shall not perish but have eternal life" (John 3:16).	● He's Alive ● Make Your Home in My Heart ● Good News ● Oh, How I Love Jesus ● I've Found Me a Treasure (add verse 4)	**Craft** Good News Treasure Pouches **Application** The colorful beads on the Treasure Pouch will remind kids of the good news that Jesus died for our sins and rose again!	**Games** ● Roll Away the Stone ● Butterfly Breakout ● Manic Monarchs ● Jungle-Bird Jiggle ● He Has Risen! **Application** Our lives can be changed because Jesus rose from the dead.
DAY 5	The Bible shows us the way to live.	Paul stands firm in his faith, even in a shipwreck (Acts 27:1-44).	"If you love me, you will obey what I command" (John 14:15).	● The B-I-B-L-E ● Got a Reason for Livin' Again ● I've Found Me a Treasure (entire song)	**Craft** Rain Forest Creatures **Application** Kids add color and "life" to Rain Forest Creatures just as God's Word adds color and meaning to our lives.	**Games** ● Man-Overboard Tag ● Out to Sea ● Snake Swap ● Crash Course ● Cargo Toss **Application** Even when life seems scary or difficult, we can have confidence that God is in control.

This chart shows you the entire program at a glance. Refer to the chart to see how your Discovery Site activities supplement other activities and help discover Jesus—the greatest treasure of all.

TREASURE TREATS	CHADDER'S TREASURE HUNT THEATER	BIBLE EXPLORATION	TREASURE TIME FINALE
Snack Peter's Adventure Cakes **Application** Peter's adventure began when he trusted Jesus. Jesus wants us to trust him, too.	**Video Segment** Chadder and his friends begin searching for a hidden treasure. They stumble onto the deck of the SS Hope, where Wally the parrot warns them to watch out for Riverboat Bob. Chadder's afraid, so Ryan, the first mate, tells him to trust God. The kids go to Whistle Cave, followed by Ned and Pete, two scraggly sailors who want the treasure for themselves. The kids find the treasure map, moments before they're trapped by a cave-in! **Application** • Where do you turn when you're afraid? • How does the Bible help you trust in God? • Mark your Student Book at a Trust Verse.	**Peter Walks on Water** • Experience being in a ship during a storm. • Try walking on "water." • Discuss how Peter learned to trust Jesus.	• Watch how a pin can go into a balloon, without popping the balloon! • Use balloons to review the story of Peter walking on the water. • Receive gem treasures as reminders that we are precious to God.
Snack Love Chests **Application** Jesus showed love for his disciples when he washed their feet. Today's snack shows that love is a great treasure.	**Video Segment** Chadder sits in an old mine car, and the car takes off, racing through the cave. Near the cave exit stands Riverboat Bob. He hits the hand brake and Chadder goes flying, right into the boxes Ryan has been stacking on deck. Chadder thinks Ryan will be mad, but Ryan says he follows Jesus' example of showing love. Chadder leaves to look for his friends, but runs into Riverboat Bob instead! **Application** • Role play how you think Ryan will react to the mess Chadder made. • How can the Bible help you when it's hard to love someone? • How can the Love Verse you highlighted help you love this week?	**Jesus Washes the Disciples' Feet** • Go on a barefoot hunt to find the Upper Room. • Have their feet washed by their Clue Crew Leader. • Help wash their Clue Crew Leader's feet. • Help one another put their shoes back on.	• See how someone shows unexpected love to the Treasure Time Finale Leader. • Receive heart locks and keys as treasures to remind them that loving actions open people's hearts.
Snack Prayer Treasure Mix **Application** Jesus' prayer teaches us to pray. The items in the Prayer Treasure Mix remind kids to pray about specific things.	**Video Segment** Chadder awakes in the mine and finds Hayley and Tim. They find a clue and decide to ask Ryan for help. The kids find Ryan in prayer, and Ryan shows them the Bible story of Jesus praying. Chadder wanders off, and Colonel Mike sees him and mistakes him for a scoundrel. Colonel Mike tells Chadder to walk the plank. **Application** • Pray in your crew for the child who'll receive your Spanish Bible. • Is there ever a time when you shouldn't pray? Explain. • How can you pray as Jesus taught?	**Jesus Prays** • Learn ways to pray for themselves. • Practice praying for various groups of people. • Create a mural with their hand prints to represent Jesus' prayer for all believers.	• Watch a skit about what it might be like for God to listen to our prayers. • Receive magnifying glass treasures as reminders that prayer brings us closer to God.
Snack Empty Tombs **Application** On the third day, Jesus' tomb stood empty. These scrumptious snacks are empty, too.	**Video Segment** Ryan explains that Chadder's a friend, and Colonel Mike points the kids toward the monkey tree. Chadder loses the map, but Ryan assures him that Jesus is the real treasure. The wind blows the map back again, and the hunt continues. The kids find the treasure chest, and Chadder finds the key to the chest hidden in the old tree. Just as they open the chest, Ned and Pete step up to steal the treasure. **Application** • How do you get to heaven? • How can knowing the treasure of Jesus change your life? • Why is it important to know about the treasure of Jesus?	**Mary Magdalene at the Empty Tomb** • Experience the sadness of the crucifixion. • Hear Mary tell how she searched for her lost treasure—Jesus—at the empty tomb. • Hear "Jesus" call their names; then draw crosses on their mural hand prints to thank God for Jesus.	• Pray; then give their sins to "Jesus" and watch as he makes the sins disappear. • Receive personal messages from their Clue Crew Leaders that Jesus loves them. • Receive three gold coin treasures as reminders that Jesus is the most valuable treasure we have.
Snack Sailboat Sandwiches **Application** When Paul faced a shipwreck, his trust in God helped him. We can live an adventurous life when we believe in God.	**Video Segment** Ned and Pete plan to take the treasure, but Riverboat Bob steps in to help. Bob reveals that he's been watching over the kids all along. Colonel Mike wants to throw Ned and Pete to the alligators, but Ryan convinces him to show God's love. Hayley, Tim, and Chadder fantasize about what they'll do with the treasure, but decide to give the money to Colonel Mike to help him bring supplies and Bibles to people along the river. **Application** • How can the Bible help you make decisions this week? • What do you think about giving your Spanish Bible away? Why? • When are times you can use the Bible verses you marked this week?	**Paul Is Shipwrecked** • Be "handcuffed," and led inside a prisoner's ship. • Hear a fellow prisoner tell about Paul's experience in the ship. • Experience a shipwreck. • Discuss how Paul's life was in God's control.	• Use a "chirping parrot" to experience the importance of working together to tell others about Jesus. • Present their Spanish translations of the Gospel of John as a special offering. • Receive a compass as a reminder that the Bible gives us direction in life.

Gearing Up for the Adventure!

GEARING UP FOR THE ADVENTURE!

Discovery Site Preparation

♣ Work with the Treasure Hunt Director to select a room for Treasure Treats service and dining. If you can't use the same room for both activities, it's a good idea to have them close by. A kitchen or uncarpeted room near a kitchen works best.

♣ Gather tables to use for food preparation and service.

♣ Inventory your church's kitchen to determine whether pitchers, paring knives, and paper goods are available for your use. If your church has these items, you can cross them off the supply list on page 14.

♣ To add rain forest ambience to your room, cover tables with green paper or boxes covered with paper to look like cargo from a ship. Set out plants and stuffed animals, tape large green paper leaves to the ceiling to look like a canopy of trees, or make up sample menus—with items such as Tree Frog Stew or Jungle Vine Salad—to post on the walls. Your menus can be as creative and outrageous as your imagination allows!

♣ Photocopy and cut out the Treasure Treats sign and arrow from the inside covers of this manual. Post these items in church hallways leading to your room. Make as many arrows as you need to guide kids to your room.

Discovery Site Supplies

Fill in the number of VBS participants you're expecting (including children and Clue Crew Leaders). Then multiply the "required amount" by the "total number of participants" to find out how much of each item you'll need.

Gearing Up for the Adventure!

FOOD SUPPLIES

	Item	Required Amount	Total Number of Participants	Total Required Amount
DAY 1	cupcakes, baked in cupcake papers	1 per participant	X _____	= _____
	whipped topping	1 tablespoon per participant	X _____	= _____
	candy orange slices	1 per participant	X _____	= _____
	Gummy Bears	1 per participant	X _____	= _____
	blue food coloring			1 small vial
	water	2 quarts for every 10 participants	# of participants ÷ 10 = ___ X 2 = ___ qts.	
DAY 2	hot dog buns	½ per participant	X _____	= _____
	strawberry preserves	1 teaspoon per participant	X _____	= _____
	cream cheese	2 teaspoons per participant	X _____	= _____
	strawberries	½ per participant	X _____	= _____
	Pull-n-Peel Twizzlers red licorice	2 strings per participant	X _____	= _____
	juice	2 quarts for every 10 participants	# of participants ÷ 10 = ___ X 2 = ___ qts.	
DAY 3	mini pretzel twists	⅛ cup per participant	X _____	= _____
	Goldfish crackers	⅛ cup per participant	X _____	= _____
	M&M's candies	⅛ cup per participant	X _____	= _____
	Gummy Bears	4 to 5 per participant	X _____	= _____
	Honey Nut Cheerios	⅛ cup per participant	X _____	= _____
	Life cereal	⅛ cup per participant	X _____	= _____
	juice	2 quarts for every 10 participants	# of participants ÷ 10 = ___ X 2 = ___ qts.	
DAY 4	Sugar cones	1 per participant, plus a few extras to account for breakage	X _____	= _____
	Oreo cookies	1 per participant	X _____	= _____
	pre-made frosting	1 tablespoon per participant	X _____	= _____
	juice	2 quarts for every 10 participants	# of participants ÷ 10 = ___ X 2 = ___ qts.	
DAY 5	pita bread	¼ piece per participant	X _____	= _____
	lunch meat	1 slice per participant	X _____	= _____
	cheese slices	½ per participant	X _____	= _____
	large pretzel rods	½ per participant	X _____	= _____
	grapes	2 per participant	X _____	= _____
	small pretzel sticks	2 per participant	X _____	= _____
	juice	2 quarts for every 10 participants	# of participants ÷ 10 = ___ X 2 = ___ qts.	

Field Test Findings

We found lots of volunteer bakers when we announced that we needed cupcakes for Treasure Hunt Bible Adventure. Senior citizens who wanted to help, but were unable to participate, loved the opportunity to serve! Ask around—you'll be sure to find plenty of help too.

A Clue For You!

When determining amounts, include Clue Crew Leaders in your head count. They'll want to taste these scrumptious snacks too!

A Clue For You!

If someone other than you is buying all the supplies, make sure to show them pictures of what the snacks look like. Then, if for some reason an item is unavailable in your area, the shopper will be able to find a good substitution.

Gearing Up for the Adventure!

Treasure Treats Service Crew

Consult with your Treasure Hunt Director to find out how many Clue Crews you'll have in your VBS. You can expect one-fourth of the total number of Clue Crews to report each day for Treasure Treats service (except for Day 1 when preschoolers will prepare treats). Multiply "per Treasure Treats Service Crew" amounts by the total number of Clue Crews you're expecting in Treasure Treats service to find out how much of each item you'll need.

SERVING SUPPLIES

Item	Required Amount	Total Number of Participants	Total Required Amount
paper cups	6 per participant	X _____	= _____
napkins	6 per participant	X _____	= _____
paper plates	3 per participant	X _____	= _____
plastic knives	2 per Mission Munchies Service Crew	X _____	= _____
shallow bowls or plates	1 per Treasure Treats Service Crew	X _____	= _____
"snackmaker" (plastic food-handler) gloves	5 per participant	X _____	= _____
pitchers	2 for every 10 participants	X _____	= _____
resealable plastic bags (sandwich size)	3 per Treasure Treats Service Crew	X _____	= _____
paring knife	1 per Treasure Treats Service Crew	X _____	= _____
large serving trays	1 per Treasure Treats Service Crew	X _____	= _____
large tub or pot	1 per Treasure Treats Service Crew	X _____	= _____
large plastic foam cooler	1 for every 50 participants	X _____	= _____
measuring scoop or clean sandbox shovel	1 per foam cooler	X _____	= _____
silver paint pen	1		
black construction paper	5 sheets for every foam cooler	X _____	= _____
aluminum foil	1 small roll for every foam cooler	X _____	= _____
bamboo skewers	5 per foam cooler	X _____	= _____
clear tape	1 dispenser for every foam cooler	X _____	= _____

A CLUE FOR YOU!
If you choose to serve juice, we recommend frozen juice. It's cheaper, lighter, and takes up less space in your refrigerator or freezer.

A CLUE FOR YOU!
The shaded items will be used to create a cool treasure chest on Day 3.

Other Supplies

○ a bamboo whistle or other attention-getting signal*
○ antibacterial soap or individually wrapped hand-wipes
○ two or three rolls of paper towels

❍ *Treasure Hunt Sing & Play* audiocassette (optional)*
❍ a chef's hat (optional)*

*available from Group Publishing or your local Christian bookstore

Discovery Site Safety Tips

♣ Always have children wash their hands thoroughly with warm water and an antibacterial soap before handling food. If you don't have time or space for kids to do this, provide hand-wipes for children to clean their hands.

♣ Instruct each Clue Crew member to wear food preparation gloves. These may be ordered from Group Publishing and your local Christian bookstore.

♣ If children have colds or other minor illnesses, have them help set up chairs or clean up the dining area rather than prepare the food.

♣ Allow only adult or teenage Clue Crew Leaders to cut with paring knives.

♣ Before Treasure Hunt Bible Adventure begins, scan the registration forms to see if any children have food allergies. Provide a suitable snack variation or alternative for children with allergies. You might keep fruit, graham crackers, or gelatin cups on hand for appropriate alternatives.

A CLUE FOR YOU!
Attention-getting signals let kids know when it's time to stop what they're doing and look at you. You can use the bamboo whistle (available from Group Publishing and your local Christian bookstore) or another noisemaker of your choice. The first time students come to your Discovery Site, introduce and rehearse your attention-getting signal. Once kids are familiar with the signal, regaining their attention will become automatic.

BIBLE POINT

✿ The Bible shows us the way to trust.

BIBLE BASIS

Matthew 14:22-33. Peter walks to Jesus on the Sea of Galilee.

When Jesus called, "Come, follow me," Peter didn't hesitate to abandon his fishing nets in obedience. As Jesus' disciple, Peter listened to Jesus' teachings, watched Jesus heal the sick, and witnessed Jesus' power over wind and waves. He believed that Jesus was the Son of God. Perhaps that's why, on the stormy Sea of Galilee, when Jesus said, "Come," Peter ventured from the safety of a boat and walked toward Jesus. The water may have been cold, the waves may have been high, and the wind may have stung his face, but Peter knew that the safest place to be was with Jesus. When Peter became afraid and began to sink, "Immediately, Jesus reached out his hand and caught him." In the arms of Jesus, Peter learned to trust. He later wrote, "Cast all your anxiety on him because he cares for you" (1 Peter 5:7).

The disciple Peter is the perfect picture of our humanity and weakness; he reminds us how desperately we need Jesus. Children feel that need just as keenly as adults. They're familiar with the fear that accompanies life's "storms"—when parents divorce, friends move away, pets die, and classmates tease. The children at your VBS need to know that, in the midst of those hard times, Jesus is calling them to "come." And when children step out in faith, Jesus will be there with open arms, ready to catch them. Today's activities will encourage children to cast all their worries upon a loving, compassionate, and mighty God.

Day 1

Treasure Treats Supplies

Today kids will enjoy making and eating Peter's Adventure Cakes. To make Adventure Cakes, you'll need:

- unfrosted cupcakes, baked in cupcake papers (1 per participant)
- whipped topping (1 tablespoon per participant)
- candy orange slices (1 per participant)
- Gummy bears (1 per participant)
- blue food coloring (1 small vial)
- paper plates (at least 1 per participant)
- paper cups (at least 1 per participant)
- shallow bowls or plates (1 per Treasure Treats Service Crew)
- napkins (1 per participant)
- snackmaker gloves (1 pair per participant)

The Treats

Today the preschoolers will be your Treasure Treats Service Crew. You may wonder whether preschoolers can make treats for the entire VBS. They can! And tackling such a big job is a great way to help preschoolers learn and understand Philippians 4:13, "I can do everything through him who gives me strength."

Here are a few tips to help you help preschoolers have a successful Treasure Treats service experience.

• Consult with the Preschool Bible Treasure Land Leader to decide whether the Treasure Treats Service Site or the preschool area would be the most conducive to preschool Treasure Treats service. If you'll be working in the preschool area, you'll need to provide trays to carry the finished treats back to the Treasure Treats Service Site.

• Consider recruiting one or two additional adult or teenage helpers. If you're working in the preschool area, you'll need help carrying the finished treats back to the Treasure Treats area. Or you may need someone to make a paper towel run!

• Allow plenty of time for preschoolers to complete the project. If you have time, take them to see the Treasure Treats Site where the older kids will be eating their treats.

Before preschoolers arrive, prepare the snack setup sites. With preschoolers, you may be able to fit two crews at each large table.

Tint the whipped topping blue—ten to fifteen drops of food coloring in each container will do the job. Gently stir the topping to blend in the color—otherwise it'll lose some of its volume. Spread the blue whipped topping onto several unbreakable plates or trays, and place one plate at each snack setup site. Place a plate of cupcakes next to each bowl of whipped topping. Place a bowl of candy orange slices and a bowl of Gummy Bears in the middle of the table.

When children arrive, have them sit on the floor. Say: **Today we're learning**

Field Test Findings

We learned that having preschoolers make the snack on the first day sets the tone for the week. Kids see that everyone can serve, no matter how old! It also sets skeptical adults at ease...when they see that preschoolers can do this, they'll realize that the rest of the week will be a snap!

A Clue For You!

Things are always a bit hectic on the first day of Vacation Bible School. Save time by putting out tubs of warm soapy water, rinse water, and paper towels or by handing out several antibacterial hand-wipes to each preschool Clue Crew leader. It's much easier than herding a lot of preschoolers into the restrooms to wash their hands.

Day 1

Field Test Findings

At first we tried this snack with unwrapped cupcakes and pre-made frosting—it was a mess! The cupcakes fell apart when we dipped them into the frosting because the frosting was too thick. At our field test, we switched to wrapped cupcakes and whipped topping—it worked great. The cupcakes tasted fantastic, too!

A Clue For You!

To help kids remember the Bible Point each day, they'll listen for you to say the Point. Then kids will respond by shouting "Eureka!" Remind kids that "Eureka!" means "I've found something valuable!"

about a man in the Bible named Peter. One night Peter had a fantastic adventure. It was a stormy night, and Peter and his friends were on a boat. There were big crashing waves on the sea that night. Let's pretend we're the sea—we'll wave our arms like waves. Show the children how to wave their arms like waves.

Peter and his friends looked out from the boat and saw someone walking on top of the waves! Walk among the children. Have the children continue to wave their arms like the waves. **It was Jesus! Jesus wasn't swimming, and he wasn't in a boat or on a raft. He was walking on top of the water, and he didn't sink!**

Put your hand on top of a child's head to indicate that he or she will act out the role of Peter. Say: **When Peter saw Jesus, he got out of the boat and walked toward Jesus. Peter walked on top of the water too.** Have Peter walk with you among the other children. Have the children continue to wave their arms like waves. Ask:

● **How do you think Peter felt when he was walking on top of the water?** (Scared; excited; happy.)

Say: **Walking on the water was an exciting adventure! When Peter trusted Jesus, Jesus helped him to walk on the water. We're going to make a snack today to remind us of Peter's adventure with Jesus. We're going to make Peter's Adventure Cakes. Peter learned that ✪ the Bible shows us the way to trust.** (Eureka!) **You can trust me now when I say that you're going to have great fun making snacks for the entire Treasure Hunt Bible Adventure.**

Hold up a cupcake, and say: **First, we need some Wave Makers. The Wave Makers will take a cupcake, turn it upside down, and dip it into the creamy blue frosting sea. The frosting will be like the waves on the sea on the night of Peter's adventure.**

Next, I'll need some Boat Makers, who will take a candy orange slice and put it on top of the waves. The orange slice looks a little bit like a boat. It'll remind us of the boat that Peter and his friends sailed on.

The next job is for Adventure Guides. Adventure Guides will take a Gummy Bear and put it on top of the waves. The Gummy Bear will remind us of Peter, who trusted Jesus one night and had the adventure of walking on top of the water. Last, we'll need some Transporters who will carry the finished snacks to the serving table. Ready!

As children work, circulate among the tables to offer help as needed. Ask:

● **What's your favorite part about the story of Peter's adventure?**

● **Jesus helped Peter walk on the water. What does Jesus help you to do?**

Encourage children who are working well together or who demonstrate kindness to each other. As preschoolers finish their jobs, have them deliver napkins and cups to the tables. Have Clue Crew Leaders pour water into the cups. Help children deliver the Adventure Cakes to each serving table.

When preschoolers are finished, say: **Today we're learning that ✪ the Bible shows us the way to trust.** (Eureka!) **Today you trusted me when I said that you'd make snacks for everyone at Treasure Hunt Bible Adventure. Look at all the snacks you made! You did a fantastic job! Thank you!**

Count out enough Adventure Cakes for the preschoolers; then take the rest of the treats back to the Treasure Treats Site.

When Clue Crews Arrive to Eat

1. Have each crew form a circle on the floor. As kids are arriving, you might ask questions such as "Are you hungry?" "What have you learned today?" or "What did you make in Craft Cave?"

2. When everyone has arrived, announce that preschoolers have prepared today's snack.

3. Have all the Cheerleaders lead everyone in cheering for the preschoolers.

4. Explain what the snack is and how it ties into the Bible story or Point.

5. Have the Prayer Person in each Clue Crew lead his or her own Clue Crew in prayer.

6. Dismiss Clue Crews to their numbered dining areas to enjoy the snack.

7. Encourage Clue Crews to stop by the preschool room and thank the preschoolers for making the snack.

When you hear your Treasure Hunt Director's signal, dismiss kids to their next Discovery Site.

✪ **BIBLE POINT**

A CLUE FOR YOU!
Since this is a pretty sweet snack, we suggest you serve water rather than juice.

A CLUE FOR YOU!
It's a good idea to have the *Treasure Hunt Sing & Play* audiocassette playing as kids enter. The lively music creates a warm and inviting atmosphere while kids wait for others to arrive.

Day 1

PREPARING FOR DAY 2

As soon as you arrive on the first day, set out the cream cheese to soften. After Treasure Treats, you can make the strawberry cream cheese filling for Day 2's snack. You may also want to cut the hot dog buns in half and pull apart the licorice strings. Wrap the buns and licorice in plastic so they don't dry out overnight. Wait until tomorrow to wash and slice the strawberries.

BIBLE POINT

✪ The Bible shows us the way to love.

BIBLE BASIS

John 13:1-17. Jesus washes the disciples' feet.

Jesus knew that his time on earth was coming to an end. His purpose would soon be accomplished, and he could return to heaven, to the side of the Father. Jesus' time with the disciples was coming to an end too. These followers, who gave up everything to follow Jesus and learn from him, must now carry his message to the world. What parting words would Jesus leave with them? How could he express his love for them and prepare them for the challenges ahead? Jesus' words were almost unnecessary, for his actions were unforgettable. The Son of God lowered himself to the position of a servant and washed his disciples' dusty feet. In this one simple act, Jesus demonstrated the depth of his love and modeled the servant's heart he desired in his followers.

It goes against human nature to put the needs of others ahead of our own. Our culture says to "look out for number one." We read magazines with titles such as Self and Moi. And we eat at restaurants where we can have it our way. Our world sends a self-centered and egocentric message to children, as well. That's why the children at your VBS can learn so much from Jesus' demonstration of love and humility. In today's activities, kids will experience the power of loving others through selfless acts. Children will discover that Jesus' actions are as unforgettable today as they were for the disciples nearly two thousand years ago.

Day 2

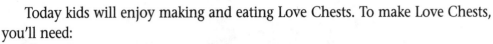

Treasure Treats Supplies

Today kids will enjoy making and eating Love Chests. To make Love Chests, you'll need:
- hot dog buns (½ per participant)
- strawberry preserves (1 teaspoon per participant)
- cream cheese (2 teaspoons per participant)
- strawberries (½ per participant)
- Pull-n-Peel Twizzlers red licorice (2 strings per participant)
- paring knives (1 per Treasure Treats Service Crew)
- a large mixing bowl
- hand-held mixer
- resealable plastic bags (1 per Treasure Treats Service Crew)
- paper plates (1 per participant)
- paper cups (1 per participant)
- juice or water
- napkins (1 per participant)
- snackmaker gloves (1 pair per participant)

Field Test Findings

Kids gobbled down these snacks—then someone told them there was cream cheese in the filling. The news caused a few kids to make faces. One girl said, "You mean I just ate cream cheese—yuck!" We decided we should have simply called the cream cheese mixture "strawberry filling." Kids loved the creamy not-too-sweet filling as long as they didn't know what was in it!

The Treats

Before kids arrive, soften the cream cheese. Put the softened cream cheese and the strawberry preserves into a large mixing bowl, and mix with the hand-mixer until well blended. If you chose strawberry jam or jelly rather than preserves, you may want to add some red food coloring to make the mixture more pink (otherwise it will look gray...most unappetizing!). Scoop the strawberry cream cheese into several resealable bags. Squish the mixture into a corner of the bag and snip off a bit of the corner to create a "pastry bag" for squirting the filling.

Day 2

Separate the red licorice into individual strings and place the strings on paper towels or plates. Cut the hot dog buns in half. Thoroughly wash the strawberries. You may also want to consider hulling and halving the strawberries. This way you don't need to put sharp knives on the setup tables.

Prepare a setup site for each Treasure Treats Service Crew. Set bags of hot dog buns, a resealable bag of strawberry cream cheese, a bowl of strawberry halves, and a plate of red licorice strings on each table.

When kids arrive, have them sit on the floor. Say: **Today we're learning that** ✦ **the Bible shows us the way to love.** (Eureka!) **In today's Bible story, Jesus showed love to his disciples by washing their feet. Today you'll show love to the rest of Treasure Hunt Bible Adventure by making snacks for everyone. The snack for today is Love Chests—they remind us that love is a precious treasure.**

Make a sample snack as you give the kids their directions. Hold up a hot dog bun, and say: **First, the Baker in your Clue Crew will take a hot dog bun, open it gently, and put it on a plate. The Baker will hand the bun to the Filling Squirter. The Filling Squirter will squirt a quarter-sized circle of strawberry filling onto one side of the bun. The Filling Squirter will hand the snack on to the Strawberry Picker. The Strawberry Picker will take a strawberry half and put it on top of the strawberry filling. See how the strawberry half looks a little bit like a heart? The strawberry is the treasure of love inside our treasure chest. Finally, the Strap Tie-er will wrap two licorice straps around the hot dog bun to look like the straps on a treasure chest. Ready?**

As kids work, circulate among the tables to offer help as needed. Ask children:
- **Why is it important to show love to people in our lives?**
- **What can you do to show love to people you know?**

When kids finish preparing the treats, go with them to deliver treats to the preschool class. Invite a Treasure Treats Service Crew member to explain the snack to the younger children. Distribute the treats, then return to the Treasure Treats Site.

Before your Treasure Treats Service Crew leaves, say: ✦ **The Bible shows us the way to love.** (Eureka!) **Making treats for everyone at Treasure Hunt Bible Adventure is a wonderful way to show love for them. Doing loving things for others makes them happy. I'm sure that everyone else at Treasure Hunt Bible Adventure will be happy to sample the tasty treats you made.**

Before kids leave, distribute any **TREASURE CHEST QUEST** Clues you've been given. Be sure to give the remaining clues to the Jungle Gym Games Leader before he or she leaves.

A CLUE FOR YOU!

Here's a no-mess way to fill resealable bags with the strawberry filling. Hold the bottom half of the bag in your fist—if you're right-handed, hold the bag in your left fist. Turn the top half of the bag inside out over your fist. Open your fist and cup the bottom half of the bag in your palm. Use your other hand to spoon the filling into the bag. When the bag is about half full, turn the top half of the bag right side out, gently squeeze out the air, and seal the bag shut.

✦ **BIBLE POINT**

TREASURE CHEST QUEST

Day 2

Field Test Findings

We were amazed at how respectful kids were of the treats made by their peers. Even when the treats didn't turn out picture perfect, children seemed to honor their friends' yummy masterpieces!

When Clue Crews Arrive to Eat

1. Have each crew form a circle on the floor.
2. When everyone has arrived, blow your bamboo whistle or other attention-getting signal, and call up the Treasure Treats Service Crew.
3. Introduce each Clue Crew by crew name or number, then have all the Cheerleaders lead everyone in cheering for them.
4. Choose a Treasure Treats Service Crew member to explain what the snack is and how it ties into the day's Bible story or Point.
5. Choose a Prayer Person from the Treasure Treats Service Crew to lead everyone in a prayer of thanks for the snack.
6. Dismiss Clue Crews to their numbered dining areas to enjoy the snack.

When you hear your Treasure Hunt Director's signal, dismiss kids to their next Discovery Site.

PREPARING FOR DAY 3

To get ready for Day 3, cut the construction paper into fourths lengthwise. Be sure to save at least one full sheet of construction paper for every treasure chest the children will make.

BIBLE POINT

✺ The Bible shows us the way to pray.

BIBLE BASIS

John 17:1–18:11. Jesus prays for his disciples and all believers, and then he is arrested.

We can only imagine the power and peace Jesus drew from his times in prayer. How he must have relished those all-too-brief moments—talking with the Father, pouring out his heart, praying for those he loved, and praising God. Perhaps that's why Jesus so often prayed privately, slipping away from the crowds to spend a few intimate hours with the heavenly Father. But this time was different. After the Passover meal, Jesus prayed, allowing his disciples to hear the burdens of his heart. And although the pain and suffering of the Cross were only hours away, Jesus prayed for his disciples and those they would lead. With his eyes turned toward heaven, Jesus spoke words of love and concern, words of finality and unity. In an intimate moment with the Father, Jesus spoke of those he loved and cared for…including you and me.

Although prayer is a key element in a child's relationship with God, praying can be difficult for children to understand or practice. Since they can't see God, children may feel confused about talking with God or disconnected when they try. That's why the kids at your VBS will appreciate today's activities. They'll learn that God really *does* hear our prayers, that we can use simple words when we pray, and that Jesus loved us so much that he prayed for us. Children will experience meaningful and creative prayers to help them discover the joy of spending time with God.

Day 3

Field Test Findings

When we field-tested this snack, we panicked because our pots of Prayer Treasure Mix didn't look like nearly enough food to feed everyone. We went through the kitchen and found extra snack items to add to the mixture. But then, after everyone had gone through the snack line, we had enough to feed everyone at least one more time. Don't worry if it looks like you won't have enough food. With the amounts listed in the supply list, there will be enough for each child to have about three-quarters of a cup of food. That's plenty—especially for small children.

Treasure Treats Supplies

Today kids will enjoy making and eating Prayer Treasure Mix. To make Prayer Treasure Mix, you'll need:

- mini pretzel twists (⅛ cup per participant)
- Goldfish crackers (⅛ cup per participant)
- M&M's candies (⅛ cup per participant)
- Gummy Bears (4 to 5 per participant)
- Honey Nut Cheerios (⅛ cup per participant)
- Life cereal (⅛ cup per participant)
- juice or water
- paper cups (2 per participant and 6 per foam cooler)
- napkins (2 per participant)
- snackmaker gloves (1 pair per participant)
- large tubs or pots (at least one for every Treasure Treats Service Crew)
- large plastic foam cooler (one for every 50 participants)
- aluminum foil (one small roll for each foam cooler)
- clear tape (one dispenser for each foam cooler)
- a pencil (one for each foam cooler)
- child's scissors (one for each foam cooler)
- black construction paper (5 sheets for every foam cooler)
- measuring scoop or sandbox shovel (1 per foam chest)
- silver paint pen
- bamboo skewers (5 per foam cooler)

The Treats

Before your Treasure Treats Service Crew arrives, prepare a snack setup site for each Clue Crew. For today's snack, some of the Clue Crews will mix the Prayer Treasure Mix; the other Clue Crews will make treasure chests to serve the snack in. For the setup site where kids will be making the snack, place packages of pretzels, Goldfish crackers, M&M's candies, Gummy Bears, and cereal on the table along with snackmaker gloves and at least one large tub.

For each setup site where kids will be making the treasure chests, place a plastic foam cooler, six paper cups, a roll of aluminum foil, and five bamboo skewers on the table. Cut four sheets of black construction paper in fourths lengthwise. Set out the construction paper strips, one whole sheet of construction paper, clear tape, a pencil, and a pair of child's scissors. Put the silver paint pen in a central location for the Clue Crews to share. Make photocopies of the "Treasure Chest Instructions" handout from pages 29-30. Put a copy of the instruction sheet at each setup site.

When kids arrive, have them sit on the floor. Say: **Today we're learning about prayer. Prayer is an incredible treasure. Any time we want to,**

Day 3

we can talk to God—the One who made the entire universe. ✵ **The Bible shows us the way to pray.** (Eureka!)

Today's snack is Prayer Treasure Mix. Some of you will make the snack today. The rest of you will make treasure chests that we'll use to serve the snack in. Let's talk about the snack first.

Everything that's in Prayer Treasure Mix reminds us of things we can pray about. The first ingredient is pretzels. They look like folded hands, and they remind us to pray. The next ingredient is Cheerios. Cheerios are little circles that have no beginning and no end. They remind us of God's never-ending love. Next comes Life cereal. It reminds us to be thankful for God's gift of life. M&M's are sweet and good. They stand for God's sweet, good blessings—the wonderful gifts God gives us. Goldfish crackers remind us that God provides the things we need, such as food. And last, the Gummy Bears look a little bit like the stained-glass windows that some churches have. They remind us to thank God for churches where we go to learn about him.

If you're on one of the snack-making crews, this is what you'll do. Each person on your crew will be in charge of adding one item to the pot. As you add your item to the pot, say aloud what your ingredient stands for. Then have everyone take a minute to pray about what that ingredient stands for. When all the ingredients have been added to the pot, take turns stirring the mixture with your hands until it's well mixed.

Send off the snack-making crews to get started on the snack. Quickly go over the "Treasure Chest Instructions" handout with the other crews. Then let them get started on the treasure chests.

As kids work, circulate among the tables to offer help as needed. Ask children:
● **When is your favorite time to pray?**
● **How do you know that God hears you when you pray?**
When the snacks are finished, have the snack-making crews find jobs cleaning

✵ **BIBLE POINT**

Field Test Findings

It helped in our test to provide kids with a recipe to help them use equal portions of the snack items among all the crews. Here's the recipe we came up with to even out the portions:
Add to each pot:
½ box Never-Ending Love
½ box of The Gift of Life
1 package Stained-Glass Windows
½ package Sweet Blessings
½ box Daily Food
2 water pitchers of Folded Hands
Take turns stirring until well mixed.

up or helping the treasure chest crews. The snack-makers can also set out napkins and empty cups for the Prayer Treasure Mix. Older children can help pour juice.

When the tables are all set up, go with the service crew to deliver treats to the preschool class. Invite a Treasure Treats Service Crew member to explain the snack to the younger children. Distribute the treats, then return to the Treasure Treats area.

BIBLE POINT

TREASURE CHEST QUEST

Before your Treasure Treats Service Crew leaves, say: ✵ **The Bible shows us the way to pray.** (Eureka!) **Today you prayed while you worked on the snack. No matter where we are or what we're doing, we can pray at the same time.**

Distribute any **TREASURE CHEST QUEST** Clues you might have, and then give the remaining clues to the Jungle Gym Games Leader.

When Clue Crews Arrive to Eat

1. Have each crew form a circle on the floor.
2. When everyone has arrived, blow your bamboo whistle or other attention-getting signal and call up the Treasure Treats Service Crew.
3. Introduce each Clue Crew by crew name or number, and then have all the Cheerleaders lead everyone in cheering for them.
4. Choose several Treasure Treats Service Crew members to each help explain one ingredient of the snack and how it ties into the day's Bible story or Point.
5. Have the prayer leaders in each Clue Crew lead their groups in prayer before the snack.
6. Dismiss Clue Crews to their numbered dining areas to enjoy the snack.

When you hear your Treasure Hunt Director's signal, dismiss kids to their next Discovery Site.

PREPARING FOR DAY 4

If you choose to make homemade frosting for Day 4, you can make that today. See the recipe on page 32. When the frosting is made, fill two resealable bags with frosting for every Clue Crew you expect in the Treasure Treats Service Crew tomorrow.

TREASURE CHEST INSTRUCTIONS

Before you begin, divide the following tasks among the children in your Clue Crew.
- **Foil Preparer**—This child will tear off long sheets of foil.
- **Tape Tearer**—This child will prepare short pieces of tape.
- **Chest Coverer**—This child will mold the foil to the cooler and tape down the edges.
- **Strap Maker**—This child will use the paint pen to put silver dots on the outside edges of the construction paper straps.
- **Lock Maker**—This child will use the pattern to make a padlock out of black construction paper.

As Clue Crew Leader, your main job will be to help the Chest Coverer cover the cooler with foil.

1. Make a false bottom for the treasure chest by putting a layer of upside-down paper cups in the foam cooler. This will keep the treasure chest from being too deep. Cover all sides of the cooler (inside and out) with foil—don't forget the lid. Tape down the edges so the foil doesn't come loose. As much as possible, crease the foil into the dips and over the ridges of the cooler. Also, make the foil as neat as possible—especially on the inside of the lid because everyone will see it.

2. Use the paint pen to put ⅛-inch diameter dots every two inches on the inner and outer edges of the construction paper strips. These dots are to resemble rivets. You'll need about eight strips with "rivets" and at least two strips without "rivets."

3. Tape construction paper strips with rivets onto the cooler and the lid as shown in the picture. Tape the other two strips onto the side of the cooler to create "handles."

4. Once all the surfaces are covered with foil and the strips are taped into place, you'll want to secure the lid to the bottom of the cooler. You'll want the cooler to be open so kids can see the treasure inside. To secure the lid, first break a bamboo skewer in half. Hold the lid of the cooler so the back edge of the lid lines up with the back edge of the cooler. Hold the lid at an angle so the chest looks open. Push the bamboo skewers into the corners of the back edge of the lid to attach the lid to the cooler. It helps to have at least two people—one to hold the lid and another to push the skewers into the plastic foam.

5. Take two full-length bamboo skewers and push them into the front corners of the cooler and the lid. This will stabilize the front end of the cooler lid.

6. Trace the padlock pattern onto black construction paper. Cut out the padlock, and outline it with the paint pen. Tape the padlock to the front of the cooler.

7. Fill the treasure chest with Prayer Treasure Mix, and look forward to Treasure Treats!

Permission to photocopy this handout from Group's Treasure Hunt Bible Adventure: Treasure Treats granted for local church use. Copyright © Group Publishing, Inc., P.O. Box 481, Loveland, CO 80539.

BIBLE POINT
✸ The Bible shows us the way to Jesus.

BIBLE BASIS
John 19:1–20:18. Jesus is crucified, rises again, and appears to Mary Magdalene.

Jesus' crucifixion was both a devastating and defining event for his followers. Although Peter, a close friend and disciple, denied knowing Jesus, Joseph of Arimathea and Nicodemus, who had been secret followers, came forward in their faith to bury Jesus. Even Mary Magdalene thought she'd lost her greatest treasure. Seeing the empty tomb, Mary probably assumed someone had stolen Jesus' body. Through her tears, she told the angels, "They have taken my Lord away, and I don't know where they have put him." Jesus, her treasure, was gone, and more than anything Mary wanted to find him. Mary didn't need to search for long. Jesus lovingly called her name, revealing himself and the miracle of his resurrection.

The greatest treasure children can find is Jesus. For in knowing Jesus, children will experience forgiveness, love, and eternal life. However, like Mary, the kids at your VBS may have trouble "seeing" Jesus. Mixed messages from the media, school, and non-Christian friends may confuse kids or mislead them. But just as Jesus called Mary by name, Jesus calls each of us by name, too. He knows the hearts and minds of the children at your VBS. Today's activities will help children discover that Jesus is the greatest treasure of all, and that he's right there, waiting for them with open arms.

Day 4

Treasure Treats Supplies

Today kids will enjoy making and eating Empty Tombs. To make the Empty Tombs, you'll need:
- sugar cones (1 per participant)
- Oreo cookies (1 per participant)
- pre-made frosting (1 tablespoon per participant)
- resealable sandwich bags (2 per Treasure Treats Service Crew)
- large serving trays (1 per Treasure Treats Service Crew)
- napkins (1 per participant)
- juice (1 per Treasure Treats Service Crew)
- paper cups (1 per participant)
- snackmaker gloves (1 pair per participant)

A CLUE FOR YOU!

You can save money by making the frosting from scratch. With an electric mixer, blend together 4 cups of powdered sugar, 1 cup vegetable shortening, and 1 teaspoon of vanilla until smooth and creamy. If the mixture is too thick, add milk one teaspoon at a time. If it's too thin, add more sugar gradually. This recipe is enough for about fifty Empty Tombs.

The Treats

Prepare a snack setup site for each Clue Crew. For each Clue Crew, fill two resealable sandwich bags with frosting. (See instructions on page 23.) At each setup site, place two bags of frosting, a plate of Oreo cookies, and a plate of sugar cones. Also set out a large serving tray for the finished snacks.

🧩 BIBLE POINT

Say: **Today we're learning that 🧩 the Bible shows us the way to Jesus.** (Eureka!) **The Bible tells us that if we believe in Jesus and in the things that Jesus says in the Bible, we'll live with him forever in heaven.** Ask:

● **What does the Bible tell us about Jesus?** (That Jesus is God; Jesus rose from the dead; Jesus did miracles.)

- **What does Jesus ask us to do and believe?** (Jesus wants us to believe in him; Jesus wants us to give our lives to him; Jesus wants us to love others and treat them well.)

Say: ✦ **The Bible shows us the way to Jesus.** (Eureka!) **Jesus came to earth to show us how to be friends with God. Jesus died for our sins so that we can have forgiveness for our sins. On the third day after Jesus died, the women went to the tomb where Jesus was buried. But the tomb was empty because Jesus rose from the dead. Jesus is alive today! We're going to make Empty Tombs for our snacks today to remind us that Jesus is alive!**

To make our snack, I'll need Cookie and Cone Counters to pair up one Oreo cookie with a sugar cone. The sugar cone will be the tomb, and the cookie will be the stone at the opening of the tomb where Jesus was buried. The Cookie and Cone Counters will hand the cookies and the cones to the Mortar Spreaders. Mortar is the stuff that holds bricks together. The Mortar Spreaders will squeeze frosting onto the Oreo cookie, covering the whole surface with frosting. The Mortar Spreaders will hand the Oreo cookie and the sugar cone to the Stone Layers, who will stick the cookie onto the opening of the sugar cone. The Stone Layers will place the finished Empty Tombs on the serving tray. Ready?

As the service crew works, circulate among the tables to offer help as needed. Ask children:

- **Why is it important to know the way to Jesus?**
- **What do you believe about Jesus?**

As kids finish their jobs, have them deliver the trays of Empty Tombs to each serving table. Have younger children count out napkins for each table. Then crew leaders and older children can come around and pour juice into the cups.

When kids finish preparing the Empty Tombs, go with them to deliver treats to the preschool class. Invite a Treasure Treats Service Crew member to explain the snack to the younger children. Distribute the treats, then return to the Treasure Treats area.

Before your Treasure Treats Service Crew leaves, say: ✦ **The Bible shows us the way to Jesus.** (Eureka!) **Jesus wants us to believe what the Bible says about him. The Bible says that Jesus is God and that he died for our sins. Our snack is an *Empty* Tomb because Jesus rose from the dead—that's something no one but God could do. The Bible shows us how to have eternal life.** ✦ **The Bible shows us the way to Jesus.** (Eureka!)

Distribute any **TREASURE CHEST QUEST** Clues you've been given. Then give the remaining clues to the Jungle Gym Games Leader.

✦ BIBLE POINT

Field Test Findings

Oreo cookies and frosting are an unbeatable combination! The Empty Tombs looked so good that the teenage kitchen helpers had a hard time resisting them before the kids came to Treasure Treats. Make enough extras for the staff to have some!

Field Test Findings

Don't use paper plates for today's treats! We found out that ice cream cones roll like crazy on plates. It's much easier to just use napkins.

✦ BIBLE POINT

TREASURE CHEST QUEST

Day 4

When Clue Crews Arrive to Eat

1. Have each crew form a circle on the floor.

2. When everyone has arrived, blow your bamboo whistle or other attention-getting signal, and call up the Treasure Treats Service Crew.

3. Introduce each Clue Crew by crew name or number; then have all the Cheerleaders lead everyone in cheering for them.

4. Choose a Treasure Treats Service Crew member to explain what the snack is and how it ties into the day's Bible story or Point.

5. Choose a Prayer Person from the Treasure Treats Service Crew to lead everyone in a prayer of thanks for the snack.

6. Dismiss Clue Crews to their numbered dining areas to enjoy the snack.

When you hear your Treasure Hunt Director's signal, dismiss kids to their next Discovery Site.

PREPARING FOR DAY 5

To get ready for the last day of Treasure Hunt Bible Adventure, use scissors to cut the pita bread into quarters. Be sure to put the pita bread back into plastic bags and close them tightly. Cut the cheese slices into triangles. Divide the cheese and the lunch meat onto plates for each snack setup site. Break the pretzel rods in half. Wash the grapes and dry them, but wait until tomorrow to slice the grapes that will be used for the preschool snacks.

DAY 5

BIBLE POINT

The Bible shows us the way to live.

BIBLE BASIS

Acts 27:1-44. Paul stands firm in his faith, even in a shipwreck.

After Paul came to believe in Jesus, he fervently shared the news of Jesus everywhere he went. In Jerusalem, Paul encountered a group of men who opposed his teachings. These men incited a riot, accusing Paul of teaching false doctrine and of defiling the Temple. In the confusion of the angry mob, Paul was arrested and thrown in prison. The following years included trials, death threats, confused centurions, secret transfers to other prisons, and finally a trip to Rome where Paul could plead his case before Caesar. As if Paul hadn't encountered enough trouble, his ship ran into a violent storm and was eventually shipwrecked! Throughout the ordeal, Paul's faith remained strong. He prayed with other prisoners, encouraged his captors to be courageous, and shared his faith in God with everyone on board. Even in the worst circumstances, Paul's life reflected the power of Christ's love.

Most of the children in your VBS won't encounter the kind of persecution that Paul faced. But they'll face tough decisions, peer pressure, false religions, and secular advice that will challenge their faith. That's why it's important for kids to use God's Word as their map for life, a tool to guide them through the storms and "shipwrecks" along the way. Use today's activities to show children the power in the Bible and to help them discover its usefulness in successfully navigating life's everyday trials.

Day 5

A Clue for You!

Be sure to get both pretzel *rods* (they're about one-quarter-inch thick) and pretzel *sticks* (they're about two inches long and very thin).

Field Test Findings

We needed to serve about two hundred people at our field test—that's a lot of lunch meat. We found that the most inexpensive way to buy lunch meat was to buy a ham and have it sliced thin (not shaved) in the deli at the supermarket. We bought a 3-lb. ham and had plenty—enough for the snack and enough to make lunch sandwiches for the staff. Also, buy sliced cheese that isn't wrapped by the slice—it's cheaper, it's quicker, and there's less plastic to throw away.

Treasure Treats Supplies

Today kids will enjoy making and eating Sailboat Sandwiches. To make Sailboat Sandwiches, you'll need:
- pita bread (¼ piece per participant)
- lunch meat (1 slice per participant)
- cheese (½ slice per participant)
- large pretzel rods (½ per participant)
- small pretzel sticks (2 per participant)
- grapes (2 per participant)
- paper plates (1 per participant)
- paring knife
- scissors
- napkins (1 per participant)
- juice (2 quarts per 10 participants)
- paper cups (1 per participant)
- snackmaker gloves (1 pair per participant)

The Treats

Prepare a snack setup site for each Clue Crew. Use scissors to cut the pita bread into quarters. Also, cut the cheese slices in triangles. At each setup site, place the pita bread, a plate of lunch meat, a plate of cheese triangles, a plate of pretzel rods, a plate of pretzel sticks, and a bowl of grapes.

Say: **Today we're learning how Paul lived for God even when things got tough!** Ask:

36

Day 5

● **In what ways did Paul show that he lived for God when he was shipwrecked?** (He encouraged others; Paul trusted that God would keep them safe.)

Say: **Paul learned to live for God by reading and studying the Bible. Then when he faced a scary situation—a storm and a shipwreck—he was able to stand firm in his beliefs and help others know that God was in control. We can learn from Paul's example by reading about him in the Bible.** **The Bible shows us the way to live.** (Eureka!) **Today we'll make Sailboat Sandwiches to remind us of Paul's adventure.**

To start off, I'll need some Sandwich Stuffers who will gently stuff one slice of lunch meat into a pita bread piece. Place the pita bread piece on a plate and hand it to the Mast Makers. The Mast Makers will take a thick pretzel rod and stick it in the pita bread piece so it looks like the mast on a boat. The Mast Makers will hand the sandwich on to the Sail Hoisters who will put a cheese triangle next to the pretzel mast. Place the cheese triangle with the flat side next to the pretzel mast so it looks like a sail. The next person in the line is the Sailor. That person will poke a small pretzel stick into a grape to make a sailor. See how the grape looks like the sailor's head and the pretzel stick is the sailor's body? The Sailor will make two pretzel and grape sailors to put in the boat. Then I'll need Transporters to take the Sailboat Sandwiches to the serving tables. Ready?

As kids work, circulate among the tables to offer help as needed. Ask children:

● **How does the Bible show you how to live?**
● **What can you do today to live for God?**

As children finish their jobs, have them help the Transporters carry the plates to the dining tables. Then instruct the Treasure Treats Service Crew to pour juice into cups and place these on the serving tables.

When kids finish preparing the Sailboat Sandwiches, go with them to deliver treats to the preschool class. Invite a service crew member to explain the snack to the younger children. Distribute the treats, then return to the Treasure Treats area.

Before your Treasure Treats Service Crew leaves, say: **The Bible shows us the way to live.** (Eureka!) **You were a great example of how to live for God while you worked hard making treats for everyone. When you come to Treasure Treats to eat, watch and see how much everyone appreciates and benefits from your faithfulness to God.**

Distribute any **TREASURE CHEST QUEST** Clues you have, and then give the remaining clues to the Jungle Gym Games Leader.

When Clue Crews Arrive to Eat

1. Divide the area where the children gather into as many sections as you had Clue Crews in the Treasure Treats Service Crew. As Clue Crews arrive, send them

Field Test Findings

At our field test, we used white bread slices instead of pita bread. We found that kids didn't eat the bread crusts and cutting the sandwiches into four triangles took a lot of time. However, white bread is less expensive than pita bread. If you'd rather use white bread, have the children make sandwiches with two slices of bread, a slice of cheese, and a slice of meat. Then cut the sandwiches into four triangles. For each sailboat, you'll need two sandwich triangles. One triangle forms the boat, while the other triangle acts as the sail. Use a pretzel mast and pretzel and grape people as in the instructions in "The Treats" section.

Day 5

Whole grapes are a choking hazard for preschoolers. At one snack setup site, cut the grapes in half. Reserve these snacks for the preschoolers.

to each section so there are approximately the same number of crews in each section. Have the Treasure Treats Service Crew gather by you.

2. When everyone has arrived, blow your bamboo whistle or other attention-getting signal, and call up the Treasure Treats Service Crew.

3. Introduce each Clue Crew by crew name or number, and then have all the Cheerleaders lead everyone in cheering for them.

4. Explain that since Paul was a missionary, the Treasure Treats Service Crews are going to go on a missionary journey to explain what the snack is today. Send out each Clue Crew from the Treasure Treats Service Crew to one of the sections, and have the children explain the snack to the Clue Crews in that section.

5. Choose a Prayer Person from the Treasure Treats Service Crew to lead everyone in a prayer of thanks for the snack.

6. Dismiss Clue Crews to their numbered dining areas to enjoy the snack.

When you hear your Treasure Hunt Director's signal, dismiss kids to their next Discovery Site.

TEACH YOUR PRESCHOOLERS AS JESUS TAUGHT WITH GROUP'S *HANDS-ON BIBLE CURRICULUM*™

Hands-On Bible Curriculum™ **for preschoolers** helps your preschoolers learn the way they learn best—by touching, exploring, and discovering. With active and authentic learning, preschoolers love learning about the Bible, and they really remember what they learn.

Because small children learn best through repetition, Preschoolers and Pre-K & K will learn one important point per lesson, and Toddlers & 2s will learn one point each month with **Hands-On Bible Curriculum**. These important lessons will stick with them and comfort them during their daily lives. Your children will learn God is our friend, who Jesus is, and we can always trust Jesus.

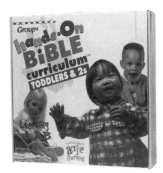  

The **Learning Lab**® is packed with age-appropriate learning tools for fun, faith-building lessons. Toddlers & 2s explore big **Interactive StoryBoards**™ with enticing textures that toddlers love to touch—like sandpaper for earth, cotton for clouds, and blue cellophane for water. While they hear the Bible story, children also *touch* the Bible story. And they learn. **Bible Big Books**™ captivate Preschoolers and Pre-K & K while teaching them important Bible lessons. With **Jumbo Bible Puzzles**™ and involving **Learning Mats**™, your children will see, touch, and explore their Bible stories. Each quarter there's a brand new collection of supplies to keep your lessons fresh and involving.

Just order one **Learning Lab** and one **Teacher Guide** for each age level, add a few common classroom supplies, and presto—you have everything you need to inspire and build faith in your children. For more interactive fun, introduce your children to the age-appropriate puppet (Cuddles the Lamb, Whiskers the Mouse, or Pockets the Kangaroo) who will be your teaching assistant and their friend. No student books are required!

Hands-On Bible Curriculum is also available for elementary grades.

Order today from your local Christian bookstore, or write: Group Publishing, P.O. Box 485, Loveland, CO 80539.

BRING THE BIBLE TO LIFE FOR YOUR 1ST- THROUGH 6TH-GRADERS... WITH GROUP'S HANDS-ON BIBLE CURRICULUM™

Energize your kids with Authentic Learning!

In each lesson, students will participate in exciting and memorable learning experiences using fascinating gadgets and gizmos. Your elementary students will discover biblical truths and <u>remember</u> what they learn because they're <u>doing</u> instead of just listening.

You'll save time and money too!

Simply follow the quick and easy instructions in the **Teacher Guide**. You'll get tons of material for an energy-packed 35- to 60- minute lesson. Plus, you'll SAVE BIG over other curriculum programs that require you to buy expensive separate student books—all student handouts in Group's **Hands-On Bible Curriculum** are photocopiable!

In addition to the easy-to-use **Teacher Guide**, you'll get all the essential teaching materials you need in a ready-to-use **Learning Lab**®. No more running from store to store hunting for lesson materials—all the active-learning tools you need to teach 13 exciting Bible lessons to any size class are provided for you in the **Learning Lab**.

Challenging topics each quarter keep your kids coming back!

Group's **Hands-On Bible Curriculum** covers topics that matter to your kids and teaches them the Bible with integrity. Switching topics every month keeps your 1st- through 6th-graders enthused and coming back for more. The full two-year program will help your kids make God-pleasing decisions...recognize their God-given potential...and seek to grow as Christians.

Take the boredom out of Sunday school, children's church, and midweek meetings for your elementary students. Make your job easier and more rewarding with no-fail lessons that are ready in a flash. Order Group's **Hands-On Bible Curriculum** for your 1st- through 6th-graders today. (Also available for Toddlers & 2s, Preschool, and Pre-K and K!)

Order today from your local Christian bookstore, or write: Group Publishing, P.O. Box 485, Loveland, CO 80539.